JOURNEY TO NATIONHOOD

...a Historical Flashback

ELDER P.O EDEM

DEDICATION

This book is dedicated to God Almighty who is the Giver and Protector of Life. All Glory to him for his continuous protection.

ACKNOWLEDGEMENT

I want to acknowledge every lover of the true Nigeria History. Those who are doing everything possible to ensure that our history is not swept away, but properly preserved.

TABLE OF CONTENT

FOREWORD

There is a thick connection between history and the future. History has a way of explaining the present and determining the future. There is no way we can keep shying away from our past and still want to get it right.

Elder P.O Edem is a creative writer and a brilliant story teller. His story-telling skills and intuitive writing was brought to the fore in this short journey into our nation's history.

As an elder who has seen much of Nigeria's chequered history, Elder Edem proffers some useful advice in tackling the nation's unstable system.

In the special feature, Ebere chuks O, a prolific writer examines the liberation struggles experienced so far in the country and the possible way forward. This is the part one of Ebere Chuks' "Nigeria and the cry for Liberation series".

This book...JOURNEY TO NATIONHOOD is a must read for all and sundry. I recommend it for youths and elders alike, anyone who truly believe in Nigeria's bright future, those who foresee a brighter day for the Nigeria nation.

CHAPTER ONE

GOVERNMENT STRUCTURE AT INDEPENDENCE

The structure of Nigerian government at independence from the colonial Britain in 1960 was as follows:

- Dr Nnamdi Azikiwe: Governor-General and later became president.
- Alhaji Balewa: Prime Minister, both at the executive level.

Dr Azikiwe's NCNC political party and Alhaji Balewa's NPC political party were in coalition or synergy with NCNC as a junior partner to NPC. The prime minister and his council of ministers (cabinet) dominated the affairs of government while the president acted as a watch dog without executive power, unlike present presidents.

- Chief Nwafor Orizu: President of the senate.

At independence, the outgoing colonial Britain gave north more seats in the federal parliament than the south put together. This means perpetual North's domination and control of Nigeria.

- Major-General Aguiyi Ironsi: was the head of the Nigerian army and the first indigenous head of the army following abrogation of existing defence pact between the colonial Britain and Nigeria.

The Judiciary continued to exist as an independent arm of the federal and the regional governments with the exclusive duty of enforcing the laws of the Nation. The regional government structure stood as outlined below:

- Dr Micheal Okpara: premier of the eastern region of Nigeria with Enugu as its capital.

- ➤ Alhaji Ahmadu Bello: premier of the Northern region with Kaduna as its capital.
- ➤ Chief Samuel Akintola: premier of the Western region with Ibadan as its capital.
- ➤ Chief Dennis Osadebay: premier of the Midwest region with Benin as its capital.

Each region had a Governor who was the ceremonial head of the regional government.

There were also regional houses of Assembly equivalent to the federal parliament. While the latter made laws on matters of federal responsibility, the former made laws related to regional governments' functions.

CHAPTER TWO

THE FIRST MILLITARY COUP IN NIGERIA

<u>CAUSES</u>

A number of unpleasant events combined to evoke the 15-1-1966 coup d'état in Nigeria. One of the incidents was corruption in form of ten percent contract kick-back and unrelenting looting of public funds which made political office holders especially ministers to live extravagant life-style at the expense of the masses they ruled. In addition, there were country-wide crises including Tiv riot of 1960-1966, western region of Nigeria and emergency rule of 1962. Others were the 1962-1963 national census controversy, 1964 federal election crisis caused by political thuggery, intimidation, murder and massive rigging which made Dr. Azikiwe, the ceremonial president to refuse to call Alhaji Balewa, the prime minister to form a new government. Further to the foregoing crises, was the 1965 Western regional election upheaval which culminated in imposition of unpopular government of NNDP political party led by premier Akintola. This political situation led to wide-spread street blood shedding and rioting in the Western region, the emergency rule in the region and persecution of leaders of Action Group Political Party led by chief Awolowo by the federal government in support of Akintola. In fact, chief Awolowo and some of his Action Group Party colleagues were accused of treason and were incarcerated by the federal regime. Some other AG leaders were marked for extermination why more others were forced to flee from the country.

The foregoing crises created a political logjam which aroused general desire and open call for change of the incompetent, corrupt and strife-promoting government.

By Major Ademoyega, one of the leading operational majors in the 15-1-1966 coup, the primary objectives of the mutiny were two fold. One was to liberate Chief Awolowo from prison and install him prime minister of the federal republic of Nigeria. The other main aim of the first military rebellion, according to major Ademoyega, was to quench the destructive and the bloody violence in the western region and the Tiv invasion by federal government security agencies and the responding hostile reactions from the native Tiv rioters who were nicknamed "the Temtios" for finding pleasure in breaking heads to pieces.

THE EXECUTION OF THE COUP

The coup which began as night-time military training code-named "Exercise Damissa", developed into a full military coup d'état. Its execution was meant to take place simultaneously in Lagos the federal capital territory and the four regional capitals of Kaduna in the North, Ibadan in the west, Enugu in the east and Benin in the Midwest of Nigeria.

Operation In North:

The execution of the coup in the north was led by Major Chukwuma Kaduna Nzeogwu who was also regarded as the leader of the coupists and planner of the coup. He was assisted by Major Tim Onwuatuegwu. Nzeogu led a group of soldiers to attack Ahmadu Bello, premier of the northern region in his residence. After killing the premier's bodyguards who came to defend the premier, wounding fatally one of the premier's wives and scattering other wives of the premier with whom she shielded their husband, Nzeogu killed the premier also. Nzeogwu and his troops killed also two other defenders of the premier inside the building. The premier's residence was bazookaed into flames, leaving a charred unidentified soldier. Nzeogwu and his soldiers went to the cantonment where they confronted

Major Hassan Usman Katsina at the OC 1 Recce squadron. Nzeogwu's soldiers also disarmed police men who opened fire on Sam Omeruos's reconciliation party and ordered the police commissioner to see Major Nzeogwu immediately. Alhaji Ali Akilu, chief personal adviser and master minder of premier Bello's schemes; Alhaji Pategi, a government driver and colonel Sodeinde were additional casualties of Nzeogwu-led operational detachment in the North. Besides, another group of soldiers led by Major Onwuatuegwu, Nzeogwu's operational deputy leader in the North, killed Brigade commander Ademulegun and his wife while capturing Katsina Ibrahim, the governor of the Northern Region. Lance corporal Lawrence Akuma, Ademulegun's house guard and two sappers of the field squadron of the NAF were also killed. In fact, the execution of the mutiny in the north led by Major Nzeogwu was absolutely successful. This made leader Nzeogwu not only to announce army take-over of the government of the northern region but also to declare martial law over the region.

Operation In Lagos, Federal Capital:

The execution of the coup in this front was led by Major Emmanuel Ifeajuna, a degree holder and international athlete, holding the commonwealth high jump record. His key assistants in the Lagos coup operation included major Wale Ademoyega, Major Don Okafor, Major Chris Anuforo and Major Humphery Chukwuka.

About 2am, Ifeajuna and some Lieutenants from the brigade headquarters went and shot Prime Minister Tafawa Balewa dead in his residence after allowing him to say his last prayer. He was shot by major Ifeajuna. Ifeajuna also killed Brigade commander Maimalari and Lt. Col. Abogo Largema, commanding officer of Ibadan-based 4th battalion. Lt. Col. James Pam, the Adjutant-General who informed GOC Ironsi about the army mutiny was abducted from his house and shot dead by major Anuforo. He also killed Lt. Col. Unegbe, the quartermaster general of the Nigerian army at the army headquarters in Lagos for refusing the coupists access to the armoury. Also killed by major Anuforo were Col. Kur Mohammed and Chief Festus Okotie-Eboh, federal finance minister.

In spite of the above high casualties, the Lagos operation failed. The execution was badly planned, coordinated and carried out. Again, there was sabotage by some of the coupists like Major John Obienu who pledged to turn up with his armoured cars for greater fire power but reneged on his promise and rather aided the federal authorities or enemies. This made major Anuforo and his colleagues to leave their assignment roles for arms from Abeokuta 2nd brigade armoury, and thereby lost the operational momentum in Lagos. Furthermore, soldiers on guard duties at the force headquarter Obalende who were meant to apprehend the fugitive GOC Ironsi did not do so. On the part of federal authorities, their access to advance leakage of the mutiny enabled the GOC Ironsi to arrange and take pre-security measures against it. Some of the precautionary actions include ordering mobile police squads to patrol the streets of Lagos, placing ban on all unauthorized organized troops movement by the cabinet office and GOC Ironsi's timely order to the 2nd Infantry battalion to quell the rebellion at all costs.

Operation At Ibadan, The Western Region Capital:

The execution of the coup in Ibadan, capital of the western region of Nigeria was led by Captain Emma Nwobosi who was assisted by 2nd Lieutenant Egbikor. The coupists began their operation by paralysing the p and T automatic telephone exchange and the city's main electrical power station to effect a total blackout. The proceeded and arrested chief Fani Kayode, deputy premier of the western region. Chief Samuel Akintola, the premier of the region who had pre-warning of advancement of his assailants, armed himself with a rifle. He fought bravely and wounded both Nwobosi and Egbikor before they killed him.

The Ibadan coup operators were later apprehended and disarmed at Ikoyi officers' mess, their operational headquarters, and taken to the Dodan Barracks in Lagos. Chief Fani Kayode was released.

Operation In Enugu The Eastern Capital:

Originally, major Chudi Sokei was designated to lead the Enugu based execution of the coup but was later posted to India for a course. He was therefore replaced by Lt. Col. Jerome Oguchi as leader of the Enugu operation.

In the early hours of January 15, 1966, Oguchi sent a small detachment to the eastern Nigeria Broadcasting Service (ENBS) to seize the station, stop the normal programme and order the broadcasters to play only military music while awaiting news from Lagos. Simultaneously, Oguchi and his troops went to premier Okpara's lodge and placed him under house arrest, deploying troops to guard the lodge. They had earlier arrested police guards at the premier's lodge and cordoned it off. Lt. Col. Oguchi then proceeded to the ENBS and made tentative announcement that the army has taken over power and continued waiting for news from Lagos. When the awaited news from Lagos revealed that the coup had failed in Lagos, Major Uko Nweze, the OC of the Enugu operational group and deputy commander the Lt. Col. David Ejoor of 1st Infantry battalion, Enugu, placed his unflinching loyalty to GOC Ironsi , traditional head of the Nigerian army. Nweze quickly released premier Okpara from the custody and recalled his troops to the barracks. The execution of the coup in eastern region of Nigeria thus became a mere caricature and complete failure.

The failure of the coup in this region is attributable to a number of factors. Principal among the causes was the general advocacy by the operational leaders for bloodless coup, which perhaps made captain Agbogu to spare premier Okpara's life when the latter defiantly disobeyed the military order to him to board army vehicle. Personal influence and plea of Governor Dr. Akanu Ibiam and the presence of President Archbishop Makarios of Cyprus, premier Okpara's guest must have played down the temper and hostility of the soldiers. Added to the above-mentioned drawbacks is major Uko Nweze, the OC of the operational group's cowardice and fearful leadership which made him to quickly switch his support to GOC Ironsi, release premier Okpara safe from custody and recalled his operational troops to barracks as mentioned before.

Midwest Regional Operation:

There was no execution of the mutiny in the mid-western region of Nigeria. Joseph Ihedigbo and his riffle company were sent to Benin, the capital of the region to arrest and detain premier chief Denis Osadebe and his regional executive council. For unknown reason, they did nothing to execute their assignment.

CRUSHING THE REBELLION

Lagos, the federal capital of Nigeria was the centre of the federal administrative power and the operational headquarter of the coupists. As said before, advance leakage of the coup to GOC Ironsi enabled him to take some pre-security measures designed to put down the rebellion. Some of the precautionary actions as mentioned earlier, include ordering mobile police squads to patrol streets of Lagos and placing ban on unauthorized organized troop movement by the cabinet office. Another action taken by the GOC Ironsi was to move out of his residence and quickly and timely rally loyal troops including the 2nd infantry battalion to quell the rebellion. The loyal troops arrested the coup leaders except Ifeajuna who fled to Ghana, while some other coupists including leader Nzeogwu voluntarily surrendered to the GOC, Major-General Ironsi.

However, following his successful execution of the coup in the Northern region, Nzeogwu took some resistant actions before his surrender on among other things, advice of Lt. Col. Patrick Anwuna. Lt. Col. Anwuna and Lt. Col. Victor Banjo had informed Nzeogwu about the complete crushing and failure of the mutiny in Lagos. As mentioned before, Nzeogwu had earlier announced by Radio Kaduna that the army had taken over the government and went on to declare martial law throughout the Northern provinces. He had also sent task forces to Jebba and Makurdi bridges on the Niger and Benue rivers respectively, to forestall possible attack by GOC Ironsi and his loyal troops. Nzeogwu sent by major Obasanjo to GOC Ironsi a 5-point conditions under which the coupists would lay down their weapons.

The condition included safety for all the mutineers, their freedom from legal action by the federal authorities, non-reinstatement of persons ousted from office, country-wide compensation for families of officers who died during the mutiny and release of all officers in custody of loyal members of the Nigerian armed forces. Infact, besides the surrender advice of Lt. Col. Anwuna and the luring tactics used by Col Comrad Nwawo from the supreme office of the GOC, Major Nzeogwu perhaps would not have voluntarily surrendered to the federal authorities. As said earlier, the most influential factor that educed major Nzeogwu to go to Lagos and surrender to GOC was the news that the GOC had orally accepted the pre-conditions for laying down arms leader Nzeogwu sent to him. Unfortunately, the GOC, as earlier asserted, reneged on his pledge after the coupists including major Nzeogwu had come into his full grip.

ADVENT OF THE FIRST MILITARY GOVERNMENT IN NIGERIA

The first but failed military coup of 15th January 1966 in Nigeria and the peaceful and voluntary handover of power by the civilian government to the armed forces paved the way for the emergence of the first military rule in Nigeria. Following the abortion of the military rebellion and the voluntary transfer of government to the army by the acting civilian president of the federation, Chief Nwafor Orizu who was also the president of the senate, on advice of council of ministers, GOC Major General Aguiyi Ironsi, head of the Nigeria army became the first military head of state of Nigeria. Dr Nnamdi Azikiwe, the substantial civilian president of the outgoing civilian administration was overseas on health ground before the coup began.

To start his military administration, major general Aguiyi Ironsi first abolished political parties and party politics throughout the country. Having become the head of the emerging military government, major general Ironsi then proceeded to appoint military governors for the four regions that then constituted the federation of Nigeria as follows:-

> Lt. Col. OdumeguOjukwu as governor of the Eastern Region with Enugu as its capital

> Major Hassan UsmanKatsina as governor of the Northern Region with Kaduna as its capital

> Lt. Col. AdekunleFajuyi as governor of the Western Region with Ibadan as its capital

> Major David Ejoor as governor of the Mid-Western Region with Benin as its capital

Unfortunately, the Ironsi-led first military government which was born in mid-January 1966 was short lived. It was terminated by a counter coup of 29th January 1966 executed by Northern soldiers executed by Theophilus Danjuma who arrested Major-General Ironsi and interrogated him on his complication in the brutal murder of Premier Ahmadu Bello. In this second nutiny in the history of Nigeria, many Southern soldiers including Major-General Ironsi were killed. He and Fajuyi, governor of the western region were murdered at the governor's lodge in Ibadan when the latter was hosting the former during the former's country-wide tour of the federation.

PUNISHMENT OF THE COUPISTS:

Although GOC Ironsi had earlier verbally accepted Major Nzeogwu's 5-points pre-condition for laying down weapons by the coupists, as mentioned before, the GOC later reneged on his promise. After he had brought the rebels under his full control by arrests and voluntary surrender, he began to punish the nabbed. Initially they were sent to the medium security prison which was usually meant for lunatics. The prison room was semi-dark, poorly ventilated and stinking. The walls were smeared with suspected faeces. There were two buckets in a room, one for drinking water and the other for faeces. Even when they were later transferred to kirikiri prison, the situation was characteristically the same.

The daily routine life of the detainees comprised jangling of keys and creaking of gates at dawn, a jogtrot or two round the lone bungalow, cold bath, breakfast at 8am, long period of language lesson in Hausa, Igbo and Yoruba, lunch at mid-day, optional break for siesta at 1:30pm, about one hour symposium at 4pm, a short break, about 45 minutes of either games or individual physical exercise or both. Others were cold bath again, dinner at 6pm and compulsory retirement to bed at 6:30pm which was dreaded and characterized by jangling of keys and creaking of gates. All the foregoing daily boring routine activities were designed to kill time and reduce pains of loneliness and idleness from normal life activities. Even Lt. Col. Banjo who was in custody for attempt to kill GOC Ironsi exploited the same loneliness, pains-reducing devices. As mentioned before, the detainees later complained to Lt. Col. Nwawo from the supreme commander's office about their problems. As a result of the detainees' complaint, they were in small groups sent to prisons all over the country where they were until the counter-coup of northern soldiers which occurred on the 29th of January 1966. Major Ifeajuna, the leader of the operational group in Lagos escaped the afore-listed punishments by, as mentioned before, fleeing to Ghana.

The victims of the counter-coup included the GOC and head of the virgin military government in Nigeria, Major General Aguiyi Ironsi, Lt. Col. Adekun Fajuyi, governor of the western region who was killed with GOC Ironsi when the latter was a guest to the former, Major Don Okafor, who was abducted from Abeokuta prison and buried alive, Major Chris Anuforo who was shot dead at Ilesha. Others were Major Obienu who sabotaged the execution of the mutiny in Lagos by failing to fulfil his promise to come up with his armoured cars for greater fire power mentioned before, Captain Isong who gave the coup ethnic coloration against the Igbo and other staggering number of soldiers from the South of Nigeria. However all coupists who were detained in the Eastern Region of the country were saved by Governor Ojukwu and his government which arrested Northerners who were resident in the region and used them for negotiation for repatriation of soldiers of Eastern origin who were still in the North.

Recorded nabbed planners and active participants of the 15-1-1966 or first military rebellion in Nigeria were as follows:-

1. Major Patrick Chukwuma Kaduna Nzeogwu:- Instructor, Nigeria Military Training College, Kaduna, who led the successful operation of the coup in the north and was widely regarded as the principal planner and leader of the first coup in Nigeria, although some people ascribe the leadership to major Ifeajuna.

2. Major Tim Onwuatuegwu:- Instructor, Nigeria Military training college, Kaduna and deputy leader to major Nzeogwu in the successful coup operation in the North.

3. Major Don Okafor:- commander, federal guard and one of the most effective operators of the 15-1-1966 military rebellion in Lagos

4. Major Chris Anuforo:- of the reconnaissance squadron and who with major Okafor performed wonderfully in the execution of the mutiny in Lagos

5. Major Humphrey Chukwuka:- of the infantry battalion and an active coupist who chased GOC Ironsi to Ikeja 2nd Infantry battalion where the GOC was telling the soldiers who were there to go to Lagos and crush the dissidents, bringing major Ifeajuna dead or alive.

6. Major Adewale Ademoyega:- of the infantry and one of the coup executors in Lagos and a graduate in history

7. Captain Emmanuel Nwobosi:- of the artillery and leader of the successful coup operation in the western region of Nigeria. He and members of his operational group were arrested at the mutineers' operational headquarters in Lagos.

8. Captain Ben Gbulie:- of the army engineers and member of the Nzeogwu-led successful coup operational group in the North who was taken to the brigade headquarters during the operation

9. Captain Oji:- of the infantry. His specific role in the execution of the coup remains unknown

10. Major Emmanuel Ifeajuna:-major of the 1st brigade, Lagos to whom some people the leadership of the first coup in Nigeria. This might be the reason why GOC Ironsi wanted the major to be brought to him dead or alive. Perhaps major Ifeajuna escaped from arrest or custody before fleeing to Ghana en route eastern region of Nigeria

WHY THE FIRST COUP WAS GIVEN ETHNIC COLOURATION AGAINST THE IGBOS

Although many northern soldiers followed major Nzeogwu in the killing of Ahmadu Bello, the premier of the northern region and sardauna of Sokoto, many

Nigerians outside the eastern region perceived the military mutiny of 15-1-1966 as Igbo plot designed for the Igbos to take over power at the federal level. Those who hold this opinion adduced a number of reasons to buttress their belief.

One of their supporting arguments is that majority of the coup planners, leaders and executors were Igbos. Another point they raised is partial execution of the coup. That whereas the original plan of the coupists was that the coup should be executed simultaneously in all the regional capitals, no proper arrangement was made to implement this intention in Enugu and Benin, hence there was no execution of the rebellion in those two regions. The ethnic colouration believers further argued that because of the partiality or tribalism in the execution of the coup, all the political leaders and soldiers except Lt. Col. Arthur Unegbe, killed in the execution were from other parts of Nigeria outside Igbo areas. They cited as example, the sparing of lives of Dr Okpara and Chief Osadebey, premier of the eastern region and the Midwest region respectively, while all their counterparts from other regions were brutally murdered.

The colourationists concluded that Dr Azikiwe, the substantive president of the outgoing civilian federal government had a hint or pre-knowledge of the coup, a privilege that made him to flee from the country before the execution of the mutiny began. They finally averred that the allegation that the 15-1-1966 military revolt was a plot by Igbos to take over the federal government was made manifest by the fact that Major-General AguiyiIronsi who became the head of the emerged military government was an Igbo man.

CHAPTER THREE

SUCCESSIVE HEADS OF STATE IN NIGERIA

➤ Dr NnamdiA zikiwe:-Civillian president and commander-in-chief of the armed forces of Nigeria, with Alhaji Abubakar Tafawa Balewa as prime minister.

➤ Major-General AguiyiIronsi;- former first indigenous head of the Nigerian armed forces who later became also the first military head of state Nigeria following the 15-1-1966 coup which ousted Dr. Nnamdi Azikiwe and Alhaji Balewa-led civilian government

➤ Yakubu Gowon:- second military head of state who was installed by the counter coup of 29-1-1966, undertaken by northern soldiers led by Theophilus Danjuma who arrested Ironsi while, as said before, the later was a guest to Adekunle Fajuyi, governor of the western region of Nigeria

➤ Murtala Mohammed:- third military head of state enthroned by the third coup led by himself which dethroned Gowon for delaying his departure from office in 1975

➤ Olusegun Obasanjo:- fourth military head of state who was installed by the fourth but failed mutiny led by Lt. Col. BukaSuka Dimka in which Murtala was killed. At the expiration of his tenure, Obasanjo handed over power to civilian rule led by Shehu Shagari in 1979.

➤ Shehu Shagari:- second civilian head of state who came to power by democratic process following the peaceful and voluntary handover of power to democratic rule by Obasanjo.

- Muhammadu Buhari:- fifth military head of state enthroned by fifth army rebellion which removed Shagari from power in 1983

- Ibrahim Babangida:- was the sixth military head of state who was brought to power by sixth coup, led by him and which toppled Buhari's government

- Sani Abacha:- was seventh military head of state installed by seventh military coup led by him and which dethroned Babangida and his government. He intended to transform himself into a civilian head of state but died naturally in office before the ambition materialized.

- Abubakar Salami:- was eight military head of state. He succeeded Abacha who as mentioned above, died naturally in office. This is the only succession to military head of state in Nigeria without coup. Like Obasanjo, Salami returned government to civilians in 1999.

- Olusegun Obasanjo:- became a civilian head of state of Nigeria following his success in a democratic general election of 1999. This election was made possible by the voluntary handover of power to democratic rule by his predecessor, Abubakar Salami. Obasanjo reigned as civilian head of state for eight years; that is from 1999 to 2007.

- Shehu Yar'Adua:- succeeded Obasanjo as civilian president of Nigeria but died in office after about or a little over two year's headship of the Nigerian nation. His vice president, Goodluck Jonathan acted for him until the 2011 general elections in which he emerged victorious as substantive president of Nigeria.

- Goodluck Jonathan:- As stated above, Jonathan became president of the nation sequel to his victory in the aforementioned 2011 general elections. After leading for his full first term tenure of four years, his bid for a second tenure flopped sequel to his defeat by Mohammadu Buhari of APC coalition.

➢ Mohammadu Buhari:- former military head of state of Nigeria emerged sixth civilian president of the country consequent upon his victorious performance in the 2015 general elections mentioned above. His anti-graft main bane of Nigeria's progress and development stance has so far won him acceptance and admiration of overwhelming majority of the Nigerian populace.

CHAPTER FOUR

OVERALL EFFECTS OF MILITARY RULE ON THE NIGERIAN NATION

There are pros and cons or advantages and disadvantages of military rule in Nigeria according to people's opinion about it. Some people feel that the coups truncated democratic rule in favour of military government which characteristically is dictatorship. They further assert that the 15-1-1966 mutiny laid the foundation of a snowball of military rebellion which was predominantly blood shedding in Nigeria for decades. This period, they further aver, being void of peace contributed immensely to retardation of development and progress of the country. The 15-1-1966 coup which was the mother of military rule in Nigeria, the anti-military rule group added, created and enhanced ethnic suspicion and consciousness in every aspect of life and relationship among Nigerians, especially in the military and politics. The cons further argue that the coup which caused the death of some political leaders and military officers from outside Igbo land evoked anti-Igbo sentiment and events. Some of the anti-Igbo feeling and occurrences included the northern soldiers counter mutiny which caused the death of Major-General Aguiyi Ironsi and a staggering number of other soldiers of Igbo Origin, the northern civilian's rioting which culminated in pogrom against Igbos resident in the north and fleeing home (South-East) of millions of survivors.

The pogrom against Igbos and inability of the federal military government led by Yakubu Gowon, a northerner, impelled Lt. Col. Odimegwu Ojukwu to declare former eastern region "Biafran Republic" independent of Nigeria. Followed by the consequent civil war which lasted from 6-7-1967 to 12-2-1970 when Philip Effiong on behalf of Governor Ojukwu who had taken asylum outside the country, announced Biafran surrender to Nigeria. Finally the cons also averred that the military rule and its product the civil war which made Nigeria to replace the Amities celebrated by the world on 11th November every year to commemorate the end of the world war I, with the armed forces remembrance day celebrated on 15th January yearly in memory of the casualties and end of the Nigerian civil war, has put Nigeria on odd position globally.

On the contrary, some people regard the emergence of military rule as a blessing to Nigeria. They regarded the termination of the incompetent, corrupt, oppressive and crises-promoting Balewa-led civilian regime as a sudden windfall to the Nigerian nation. Closely related to this, according to them is the liberation of the victims of ousted civilian government's oppression which comprised, among other things, vindictive imprisonment and arbitrary detention. The pros also claimed that advent of military rule in Nigeria restored normalcy in strife-torn western region of Nigeria in Particular where political thugs and general civil rioting reigned supreme and took toll of lives and properties, owing to election rigging and imposition of unpopular government on the region. The pro-military rule in Nigeria also claimed that the pre-emptiness of the northern Muslim leader's threat of "dipping the sword in sea" was brought about by the advent of the military intervention in the government of the Nigeria nation.

CHAPTER FIVE

THE NIGERIAN CIVIL WAR

THE CAUSE

A chain of events successively and eventually led to the civil war between the then eastern region (Biafra) and the rest of Nigeria in 1967. The 15th January, 1966 military mutiny which was led mostly by Igbo majors and involved killing of some northerner political leaders and military officers laid the foundation of disastrous civil war. The news about murder of their leaders in the first military rebellion evoked wide-spread rioting and violence among the northerners. They resorted to unrestrained mass slaughtering (pogrom) of Igbos resident in the north, forcing survivors to flee home (eastern region).

Furthermore, northern soldiers plotted and executed a counter coup of 29th July 1966 in which they killed a staggering numbers of soldiers of Igbo origin including Major-General Ironsi whose military government was also terminated by the counter coup. Even some of the soldiers of Igbo origin who were in detention in prisons for their participation in the first military rebellion, were also among the Igbo casualties of the counter coup. For example, Major Okafor was abducted from Abeokuta prison and buried alive by the northern counter coupists.

However and as mentioned earlier, all who were lucky to have been detained in the eastern region were saved by Governor Ojukwu and his government. The governor and his government then arrested northern residents in the region and used them for negotiation for repatriation of soldiers of eastern region still trapped in the north. Under the foregoing unsafe circumstance for Igbos in particular and people of eastern region origin in general in Nigeria, and the inability of the federal government to protect them , Governor Ojukwu was constrained to declare eastern region Independent Republic Of Biafra. General Gowon, the new military head of state of Nigeria, having failed to prevent the cessation bid of eastern region by hurriedly splitting Nigeria into twelve states, attacked it and thus ignited the civil war in Nigeria.

THE EXECUTION

Following the declaration of Biafra independent from Nigeria by Governor Ojukwu, the federal military government under the leadership of General Yakubu Gowon attacked Biafra, as stated before. Within a year, the federal government troops surrounded Biafra and captured the coastal oil facilities, including the city of Port Harcourt. In addition, the federal authority imposed on Biafra total blockade which caused severe famine which in turn caused demise of about two million civilians via starvation and resultant diseases. The pressure mounted on Biafra by the superior military power of the federal government and the unbearable economic hardship to which Biafrans were subjected by the blockade, impelled the Biafra leadership and troops to surrender to the federal government after about three years' gallant fight. The surrender was announced on behalf of governor Ojukwu who had taken asylum outside the country. The civil war which started on 6th July 1967 thereby came to an end on the 12th of January 1970, although the end of the hostility was formally announced on 15th January 1970 by General Gowon, the then military head of state of Nigeria.

The starvation and its tragic effects on Biafran civilians incurred the sympathy of international non-governmental organizations which brought relief aids to the starving Biafran citizens throughout the period of the war. While France in some respects supported Biafra, it nevertheless with Israel supplied weapons to both sides in the conflict. On the other hand, Britain the ex-colonist of Nigeria and Soviet Union were the backers of the federal military government then based in Lagos, former capital of the Nigerian nation.

THE AFTERMATH ON IGBOS

Since the end of the civil war, the Igbos have been neglected to the background of the affairs of Nigeria despite the fact that Igbo leaders dead and living like Dr. Nnamdi Azkikwe, played a dominant and front-running role in Championing the bid of Nigeria to liberate itself from the undemocratic, dictatorial and exploitative colonial rule of Britain. For example, Enugu the capital of the former eastern region has since been replaced with Port Harcourt while the apex national position of president or head of state of Nigeria has since the end of the civil war in 1970 eluded the Ibos who constitute one of the three major ethnic groups in the Nigeria nation.

MY ADVICE

Nevertheless, I enjoin the Igbos to shelve permanently the agitation for separate existence of South-East zone or former eastern region from Nigeria and eschew any form of violence or rioting based on this quest. They should rather harness, strengthen and maximally and fully continue to exploit their God-given enterprising, entrepreneurial, inventive and creative talents and potentials to actualize their individual and collective life ambitions. This is a divine will for them and more profitable than cessation. In addition, they should through their accredited and peace-loving leaders or representative continue relentless to dialogue with the federal authorities to erase palpable injustice meted out to them or their zone by any federal regime, past or present.

However, Edda clan in Afikpo South Local Government Area of Ebonyi state has an adage which says, *"Oduakwaduaowu"*. This means that whoever advices a weeper to stop weeping should also exhort the mourner to cease lamenting, In the same vein, I fervently implore all federal authorities to refrain from dichotomy, ethnicity, sectional interest or domination, discrimination or marginalization and all other forms of injustice in their governance of the Nigerian nation. Our omnipotent creator and providence to whom all humans are accountable, commands that we do to others as we would like others to do to us. Moreover, the forgoing anomalies inevitably breed resentment which often culminates in violent reactions and lack of peace, especially in multi-ethnic country like Nigeria. A nation void of peace is undoubtedly and unavoidably bereft of progress and development as well as general welfare and happiness of its citizens. Nigeria as a nation is an indivisible entity. Consequently, anything that affects any part of it impacts on the whole directly or indirectly.

I further suggest that certain divisive and friction-provoking elements in the Nigerian governance should urgently be addressed. Some of them are the apex positions of the three arms of the federal government. They include President or Head of State, Senate President, Speaker of House of Representatives and the Attorney-General/Minister of Justice of the Federation. These vital posts should invariably rotate among the six geo-political zones of the country in a manner that prevents concentration of two or more of them in one zone, neither north nor south of the nation is ever void of persons capable of national leadership. Undoubtedly, such concentration of apex national posts tantamount to a dummy of re-colonization of Nigeria by the dominant zone or section of the country.

Furthermore, for proper and efficient national planning, equitable representation and distribution of national resources or commonwealth, exact population of Nigeria must be ascertained and obtained. This calls for a national consensus devoid of politicization, falsification, manipulation and any other fraudulent practices. Again, the peculiar and globally unprecedented proliferation of political parties in Nigeria is not only odd, ridiculous and laughable but also a deliberate invitation to anarchy in the nation's governance. Which other country in the world has twenty or more political parties besides Nigeria? Finally, the constitution which is the final arbiter of governments and the citizen's actions should be a reflection of popular opinion of the Nigeria populace, expressed through their accredited representatives.

CHAPTER SIX

BOKOHARAM AND MAITATSINE SECTS

BOKO HARAM

THE ORIGIN

Between 2005 and 2009, a hard-line Islamist sect established itself at a compound in Maiduguri's railway district. The sect known as "Boko Haram" which means "western education is forbidden" gradually brought more and more people under its influence. Among its ranks were people from all levels of the society, including street kids, traders, discontented non-loyal students and wealthy business men. Many of the young men and women members came from the University of Maiduguri where elites of the 1990s sent their children to be educated. The university was famous for the hedonism of its students who indulged in ritual and display of wealth, being children of the wealthy elites who made money during the oil boom of the 1970s.

Discontented students and university dropouts moved to the youth wing of a salafi group at a mosque in Maiduguri. These included sons and close relations of the state governor, state secretary and prominent business men. The salafists preached that spiritual corruption was the cause of Borno's ills. On joining the salafists many of them burnt their university certificates.

HOW YUSUF BECAME LEADER OF BOKO HARAM

Mohammed Yusuf saw potential of these young radicals who were born into privilege. He had been travelling around northeast preaching, making contacts and winning followers since mid-1990s. He was a charismatic preacher who easily attracted audience. His radical ideas about the infidel state of Nigeria resonated with many people. From being one of thousands of Almajiri children (i.e. religious students who begs on street for a living), he emerged leader of youth wing of the Salafist group at Maiduguri's popular Alhaji Muhammadu Ndimi mosque. Yusuf taught his followers that Muslims who participated in any form of democratic system of government were apostates and should be killed by the faithful. Furthermore, that the wellspring of corruption was the education put in place during and after the colonial rule by Christian Britain. Before the 2009 uprising, Yusuf's influence had spread deep into the border region.

BOKO HARAM'S CONFLICT WITH GOVERNMENT

Boko haram's present conflict with the government began on 20th February, 2009. On that day, a large group of members of the sect were travelling for a funeral by many motorcycles. A dispute arose between the police and the sect over latter's refusal to wear mandatory helmets. In the ensuing strife, several members of the sect were shot dead or wounded by the police. In the weeks following the encounter, leader Yusuf made series of inciting widely-circulated speeches, calling in Muslims to prepare for a Jihad to fight the infidels for Allah's sake. In response to the threat, government order the police to raid Yusuf's large farm which was his base in Bauchi. In the assault, hundreds of the sect members were captured while several more were killed. The police also laid siege to the sect's headquarters in the Ibn Tamiygah mosque compound in Maiduguri.

When they perceived that the state forces had pulled back and were shooting at them from a distance, the sect began to roam the streets of Maiduguri for four days, killing police, soldiers and scores of civilians within their reach. When the authorities re-established its control of the town, Yusuf was captured by soldiers and handed over to the police who shot him dead. Seven years after Yusuf's death (2016), the war between the Nigerian state and boko haram has continued, changed and developed. From late 2014 to early 2015, the sect controlled estimated 70% of Borno state which the previous and present federal governments have been relentlessly striving to reclaim. Fortunately, by August 2015 under Buhari-led federal government, the military had reversed many of the sect's gains by pushing it back to more remote areas. But the war continues as the sect has resorted to suicide bombing and seek-and-hide tactic while skirmishes in border regions continue in the north-east of Nigeria. Another outstanding problem of the government in the war is location and rescue of the persons including 219 Chibok school girls who were abducted on 14th April 2014 by the sect. By continued serious concern of the federal authorities on the conflict and the abducted, it is optimistically hoped that the destructive fanatical religious extremists and hooligans would be eventually completely eradicated.

Similar to boko haram was Maitatsine sect which emerged earlier in early 1980s in the predominantly Muslim Kano State and was led by Mohammed Marwa, a radical Islamic preacher. His Hausa nickname means "the one who damns". He declared that reading of books is a hell-assured crime in the eyes of Allah. The sect also warred against modernism. They waylaid passenger vehicles, railway trains, killed some of their passengers and preserved some others for manual labour. The sect also took women and children captives for household chores and sexual slavery in their enclave. The enclave was located in the heart of Kano city which is now the second largest metropolis in Nigeria. Their primary targets were their fellow Muslims even before the "infidels". The Maitatsine sect was also anti-modern luxuries like radio, television, watches, motor cars and the like. Hence they hacked motorists to death or burned them in their vehicles.

During their developments, political aspirants including Governors courted them and turned blind eye to their violence and increasing fortified enclave or territory takeover. Some even donated money to the sect. The maitatsine movement therefore progressed with impunity and grew stronger while their leader was trumpeted as the last Imam (leader of prayer in a Muslim mosque).

<u>MAITATSINE SECT ENCOUNTER WITH GOVERNMENT</u>

When the sect made their move, they routed the police and frustrated the military. Only the Nigeria Air Force bombs could dislodge them from their enclave and rout them. The enclave was a scene of fortifications and blood, as well as headless remains of their victims. In Comparism, The social theology and ideology of the Mohammed Yusuf-led Bokoharam sect and those of the Mohammed Marwa-led Maitatsine sect differed only in detail and origination. Generally, both leaders and their followers encouraged anti-democratic government and lawlessness. They were also against freedom of worship and championed religious bias. The two sects took great delight in brutal killing or enslaving of their victims and thrived on impunity in the criminality. Education and other forms of modernism were abomination to the two Muslim sects.

NIGERIA AND THE CRY FOR LIBERATION
BY
EBERE CHUKS O.

Nigeria as a nation came into existence in 1914 as a result of the amalgamation of the northern and the southern protectorate of the old British colony by Lord Lugard. From then on, the two different protectorates with diverse ethnic groups began to integrate into the new system; they started to learn the process of living together as one. The development stage was not easy but with time, the adhesive and cohesive forces grew stronger. 46 years later, the new nation was now ripe to have their destiny in their own hands.

Following years of nationalistic independence struggle, the young nation was finally handed over the realms of power, to direct their own affairs. Drums were rolled out, red carpet was laid and there was a loud ovation as Nigeria got her independence on October 1st, 1960. The independence was well celebrated as they believed that they could manage their nation better on their own. Eyes all over the world were on the young Nigeria, as they looked on for deeper unity in this culturally and ethnically diversified nation. Despite the outer feeling of oneness, the seeming show of "All is fine" and the immediate glee at self-rule, there were still internal murmur, inherent uneasiness and growing tension. Crisis erupted, from political to sectarian and to then to ethnic bigotry. It became evident that the nation was now sitting on a 'time bomb' as the time ticks away. Desperate attempts were made at deactivating this time bomb but to no avail until it finally exploded in 1967 when the struggling nation was thrown into three years of bitter civil war. The war raged on for three terrible years before the towel was finally thrown in 1970. This three years unarguably was one of the most terrible and devastating period of Nigeria's history. A war which saw millions of lives lost and million-worth of properties destroyed. Young future fathers were massacred, women were left childless and children rendered parentless while many others were starved to death. Probably what is of more concern is the cause of the war, so as to avoid a possible re-occurrence.

A part of the nation (the eastern region) tried to secede, over alleged discrimination, pogrom and non-challant attitude of the central government to the eastern region. After the war ended in 1970, the seceding nation, 'Biafra Republic' was re-integrated as the eastern region of Nigeria. Till today, the eastern Nigeria still feels very much marginalized as they are still not enjoying an equal share of the 'federal cake'. This has led to recent agitations such as resuscitation of the Biafran struggle and the Niger-delta militancy struggle. What then can be done to checkmate these constant divisive tendencies and the loss associated with it? A trace down memory lane should be made to identify how it all began, the cause and the likely way out. The Biafran secession and the attendant civil war was well pronounced and brought ethnic /regional liberation struggle to the fore. But that was actually not the first liberation struggle to be seen in Nigeria since the Briton left the shores of the Nation. It has been insinuated that the Northern region initially intended to secede from Nigeria after they successfully carried out the July 1966 counter-coup. But they were dissuaded against that decision.

Perhaps what may be termed the first armed insurrection and liberation struggle in post-colonial Nigeria started in February 23, 1966 when a group of Ijaw youths led by Major Isaac Jasper Adaka Boro declared the 'Niger Delta Republic'.

Their Aggression?

The exploitation of oil and gas resources in the Niger Delta areas which they said benefitted only the federal government of Nigeria and eastern region with capital in Enugu and nothing left for the Ijaw people.

An undergraduate student of chemistry and student union president at the University of Nigeria, Nsukka, Adaka Boro left school to lead an armed protest against the injustice melted on his people by the government in power. He believed that the people of the area deserve a fairer share of proceeds of the oil wealth. He formed the Niger Delta Volunteer Force (NDVF), an armed militia with members consisting of his fellow Ijaw ethnic group.

"Today is a great day; not only in our lives, but also in the history of the Niger Delta....This is not because we are going to bring the heavens down, but because we are going to demonstrate to the world what and how we feel about oppression... Remember your 70-year old grandmother who still farms to eat, remember also your poverty-stricken people and then remember too your petroleum which is been pumped out daily from your veins, and then fight for your freedom!"

With these tender but effective words, Boro committed his 159-member militia to a battle of unlikely outcome. They gallantly battled the federal forces for twelve days but they were finally routed by the far superior federal firepower. Boro and his compatriots were tried for treason and condemned to death. However, the federal regime of Gen. Yakubu Gowon came into power and the sentence was reverted to life imprisonment. They were finally granted amnesty on the eve of the Nigerian civil war in May 1967. Adaka Boro then enlisted and was commissioned as a major in the Nigerian army. He fought on the side of the federal government but was killed under mysterious circumstances in active service in 1968 at Ogu, near Okrika in Rivers State.

Isaac Adaka Boro is still remembered by his people as a hero, who fought against oppression and stood for justice; a true voice who only echoed their cry for freedom and liberation...

Ebere Chuks O. is a prolific writer and a social commentator. This is the first (introductory) part of his series on "Nigeria and the cry for Freedom".
You can check Ebere Chuks on **Facebook**: https://facebook.com/patebere1, **Twitter** @patrickebere, LinkedIn: Ebereedem

ABOUT THE AUTHOR

Elder P.O Edem is a brilliant story teller and a writer per excellence. As a retiree, he has spent the later days of his life on useful research and educative writings.

Elder Edem has a Bachelor's degree in Business Education and Masters Degree in Educational Administration and Planning. Having been a civil servant, Elder Edem retired from active service in 1994.

He is blessed with three wonderful children, two sons and a daughter.

ADVERTISEMENT